DOG ON BOARD

The True Story of Eclipse, the Bus-Riding Dog

by **Dorothy Hinshaw Patent** and **Jeffrey Young**
photographs by **William Muñoz**

CROWN BOOKS for YOUNG READERS
NEW YORK

My name is Eclipse, and I live in Seattle with my buddy Jeff.

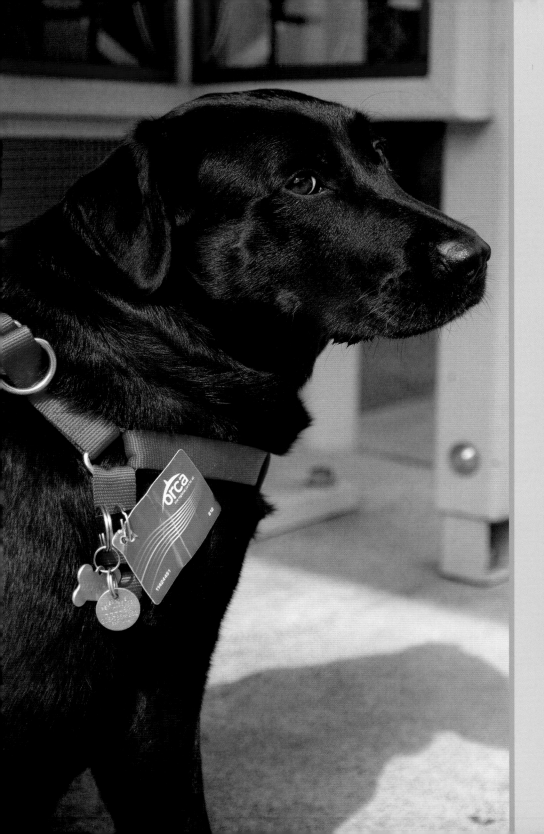

Almost every day, we take the bus to my favorite place, the dog park. The drivers know me, and I know them. I even have my own blue bus pass.

One day, I was waiting with Jeff at the bus stop when our big red bus showed up. Time to go to the park! I just hopped on board without checking to make sure Jeff was behind me.

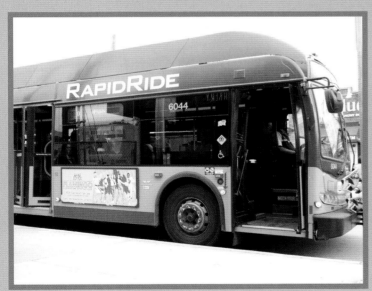

It turned out Jeff had missed the bus. But of course, I got off at the dog park—that's where we were going, after all. Luckily, a friend at the park opened the gate and let me in.

Soon I was romping with my doggie buddy Lyla.

Where was Jeff? I wanted to play ball with him.

Meanwhile, Jeff was really worried about me. After looking around the bus stop and our neighborhood, he jumped on the next bus and rushed to the dog park, hoping I was there.

Boy, was I glad when Jeff showed up! I thought he'd gotten lost.

After that, sometimes I'd go ahead on the bus on my own if Jeff was busy. I'd sit with new friends on the bus, or just by myself.

But I always got off at the dog park, where Jeff would meet up with me.

Then, one day, everything changed. TV reporter Lindsay Cohen found out I knew how to take the bus to the park by myself. Lindsay's news story made me famous. Now we're buddies, so she comes to see what I've been up to.

Before long, people were stopping me and Jeff on the street, asking if I was the dog on TV. They wanted to meet me and have their picture taken with me.

Even though I'm a celebrity now, Jeff and I still have fun riding the bus around town. I love going to the park, because I always find some new playmates there.

The dog park is usually only our first stop. After we're done playing, we head to my favorite store, Mud Bay, where I can get some cold water to drink and then take a look around.

THANKS FOR THE TREAT!

Then it's on to Pike Place Market.
It smells *so* good I can hardly stand
it. Fish, cookies, and more all mixed
together.

WHAT A
SMELL-O-RAMA!

Since I love riding the bus, I thought a ride on the Ferris wheel would be fun, so up we went!

UH-OH.
IT'S A LONG
WAY DOWN!

What's next? Hmmm . . . I wonder what it's like to go up the Space Needle elevator. Jeff and I could ride all the way to the top.

Or maybe we'll take a ferry ride!

Wherever we go and whatever we see, as long as I have my buddy Jeff to share the ride, I'm happy.

A Note from Jeff

Eclipse, a "Mastador" (half Labrador retriever and half mastiff), was born on a farm outside Hoodsport, Washington. My son, Brandon, worked odd jobs on the farm to "pay" for her. Every day, Eclipse would meet him as soon as he got off the bus from school, and they would play, walk, and hang out until bedtime. Eventually, football began to take up more and more of Brandon's time, so he dropped off Eclipse with me in Seattle for what was supposed to be "just till the end of football season, okay, Dad?" But when her first birthday came around, it became clear that Eclipse's visit had become an adoption.

Seattle is a very dog-friendly city, but Eclipse had to learn to be an urban dog. Lessons, practice walks, and lots of reward treats and hugs helped Eclipse become "street-smart." Being such a fast learner also helped her find the way to the dog park by herself one winter day. Eclipse's bus adventures have given her many admirers, including a local group of commuters called Ecliptomaniacs, who spoil her with attention.

Sometimes worried bus riders see her on her own and call the phone number on her name tag. In the past, I might have been on the next bus when I got these calls. Now that she's so famous, I stay on the same bus, but still give her room to make new friends on her own. Eclipse and I are pretty good at keeping each other in view. But even when we can't see each other, we are in tune. Sometimes it's not just the notes that make up a great song; it's the spaces in between as well.

A Note from Dorothy & Bill

Meeting Jeff and Eclipse and working with them on this book have been a real joy—they're a great team. Seattle allows dogs on its city buses, and since Eclipse is a registered service dog, she's allowed to go wherever Jeff goes.

You can keep in touch with Eclipse and her activities through her website and her Facebook page.

eclipseattle.com

facebook.com/eclipseaRider

Eclipse's story was watched and shared by millions of viewers! Here are links to some of the most popular videos:

The original news story from KOMO-TV in Seattle that started it all:

komonews.com/news/local/Seattle-dogs-rush-hour-ride-on-the-bus-by-herself-weekly-288345081.html

To see the follow-up story about Eclipse's instant fame, go to:

komonews.com/news/local/A-pooch-with-paparazzi-catching-up-with-Eclipse-the-bus-riding-dog-288626101.html

"Eclipse the Bus-Riding Dog's Day Off in Seattle"

youtube.com/watch?v=vLVKVPc_Z6k

There are too many articles and videos about Eclipse to list them all. Here is a sampling:

abcnews.go.com/WNT/video/dog-seattle-takes-bus-visit-dog-park-28208203

insider.foxnews.com/2015/01/13/seattle-dog-learns-how-ride-buses-takes-trips-alone-dog-park

today.com/health/pup-lic-transportation-seattle-mutt-takes-solo-bus-rides-dog-1D80424003

To my husband, Greg, who enjoyed exploring
Seattle with Jeff and Eclipse as much as I did.
—D.P.

To Eclipse and the independent spirit of dogs.
—J.Y.

To the memory of my mother, who had a
lifelong love of libraries and books.
—W.M.

Acknowledgments

The authors would like to thank Lindsay Cohen
and Eric Jensen of KOMO-TV for their help and
continued interest in Eclipse. Thanks also to the
people at Mud Bay, who always make sure Eclipse
gets fresh water to drink and at least one treat when
she visits, and to Sarah Love and the children—Skye,
Verrity, Cedella, Melanie, and Jude.

Jeff also thanks Brandon Young for leaving Eclipse
so long that the babysitting gig became an adoption,
and Lauren for relentless, repetitive lessons in urban
navigation that turned out to be a blessing for a spirited
canine like Eclipse. Also thanks to the King County
Metro Transit, for giving Eclipse the chance to show
what a gem a well-behaved off-leash dog can be,
and to all the Ecliptomaniacs!

Text copyright © 2016 by Dorothy Hinshaw Patent and Jeffrey Young
Jacket photograph copyright © 2016 by Julie Austin
Julie Austin photographs copyright © 2016, page 4, page 13 top left,
page 14 bottom, page 15, page 17 top and bottom, page 18, page 25.
KOMO-TV photographs copyright © 2015, pages 20 and 21 (top). All other
photographs copyright © 2016 by William Muñoz.

Visit us on the Web! randomhousekids.com
Educators and librarians, for a variety of teaching tools, visit us at
RHTeachersLibrarians.com
Library of Congress Cataloging-in-Publication Data is available upon request.
ISBN 978-0-399-54988-5 (trade) — ISBN 978-0-399-54989-2 (lib. bdg.) —
ISBN 978-0-399-54990-8 (ebook)

MANUFACTURED IN CHINA
10 9 8 7 6 5 4 3 2 1
First Edition